IF YOU WERE A KID AT THE
DECLARATION OF INDEPENDENCE

BY SONIA W. BLACK • ILLUSTRATED BY LEO TRINIDAD

CHILDREN'S PRESS®
An Imprint of Scholastic Inc.

Special thanks to our consultant, Dr. Le'Trice Donaldson, assistant professor of history at Auburn University, for making sure the nonfiction text of this book is authentic and historically accurate.

NOTE TO THE READER, PARENT, LIBRARIAN, AND TEACHER: This book combines a historical fiction narrative with nonfiction fact boxes. While all the nonfiction fact boxes are historically accurate and true, the fiction comes solely from the imaginations of the author and illustrator. The author and the editors acknowledge that, during this same time period, the experience of kids from races, ethnicities, and/or backgrounds other than the ones featured was extremely different.

Copyright © 2025 by Scholastic Inc.

All rights reserved. Published by Children's Press, an imprint of Scholastic Inc., *Publishers since 1920*. SCHOLASTIC, CHILDREN'S PRESS, and associated logos are trademarks and/or registered trademarks of Scholastic Inc.

The publisher does not have any control over and does not assume any responsibility for author or third-party websites or their content.

No part of this publication may be reproduced, stored in a retrieval system, or transmitted in any form or by any means, electronic, mechanical, photocopying, recording, or otherwise, or used to train any artificial intelligence technologies, without written permission of the publisher. For information regarding permission, write to Scholastic Inc., Attention: Permissions Department, 557 Broadway, New York, NY 10012.

Library of Congress Cataloging-in-Publication Data available

ISBN 978-1-5461-3616-3 (library binding) / ISBN 978-1-5461-3617-0 (paperback)

10 9 8 7 6 5 4 3 2 1   25 26 27 28 29

Printed in China 62
First edition, 2025

Book design by Kathleen Petelinsek

Photos ©: 9: Nikreates/Alamy Images; 11: Shutterstock; 13: Rare Book Division/The New York Public Library. "Common sense: addressed to the inhabitants of America" The New York Public Library Digital Collections. 1776.; 15: Look and Learn/Bridgeman Images; 17 all: Don Troiani. All Rights Reserved 2024/Bridgeman Images; 19: Shutterstock; 21: GraphicaArtis/Getty Images; 23: NPS Photo; 25: National Archives; 27: William Walcutt/Wikimedia.

TABLE OF CONTENTS

A Different Way of Life................ 5

Meet Henry!............................. 6

Meet Lavinia and Isaac!............ 7

Map....................................... 28

Timeline................................. 29

Words to Know...................... 30

Index..................................... 31

About the Author................... 32

About the Illustrator............ 32

A Different Way of Life

In the early 1700s, the United States was not made up of 50 states like it is today. There were only 13 **colonies**. The colonies were ruled by King George III of Great Britain and the British **Parliament**. They made many laws the colonists felt were unfair. The colonists were divided. Some, called loyalists, trusted British rule. Others, called patriots, wanted to make their own laws. Eventually, the patriots **rebelled**. They formed **militias**, later joined together as the Continental Army, and fought the powerful British Army in the American Revolutionary War (1775–1783). The French helped the Continental Army by providing training, weapons, and other goods. If you lived during the summer of 1776, you would have heard big news of the Declaration of **Independence**. Written by a committee of colonial leaders, this document officially declared America's independence from Great Britain. Turn the page to visit this important time in American history!

Meet Henry!

Henry Lewis lives with his parents on a wheat farm in the New York colony, near the island of Manhattan. Henry loves to have fun and is very creative. He loves to tinker with materials like sticks and strings to make all kinds of things. Sometimes he enjoys playing pranks on people.

Meet Lavinia and Isaac!

Lavinia Alden and Isaac Douglas are Henry's friends. Lavinia lives in the farmhouse next door. She's full of energy, always daring to outdo her friends at one activity or another. Lavinia also loves to play pranks on people.

Isaac's family owns a blacksmith workshop nearby. He often wanders off by himself to go fishing, but he also enjoys hanging out with Henry and Lavinia. Isaac is never without his favorite toy, a whistle his father made for him on his birthday.

It was June 1776 in the New York colony. The war with Great Britain was ramping up. British soldiers regularly **patrolled** the streets. On the Lewises' farm, after a long, hot day, chores were all done. Henry and his parents sat down to eat supper. Suddenly, there was loud pounding at the front door!

BANG! BANG!

"Open up!" a voice bellowed.

"Now!" another voice demanded.

"British soldiers . . ." whispered Mr. Lewis.

Sensing trouble, Mr. Lewis told Henry to run to the neighbors' farm and stay there.

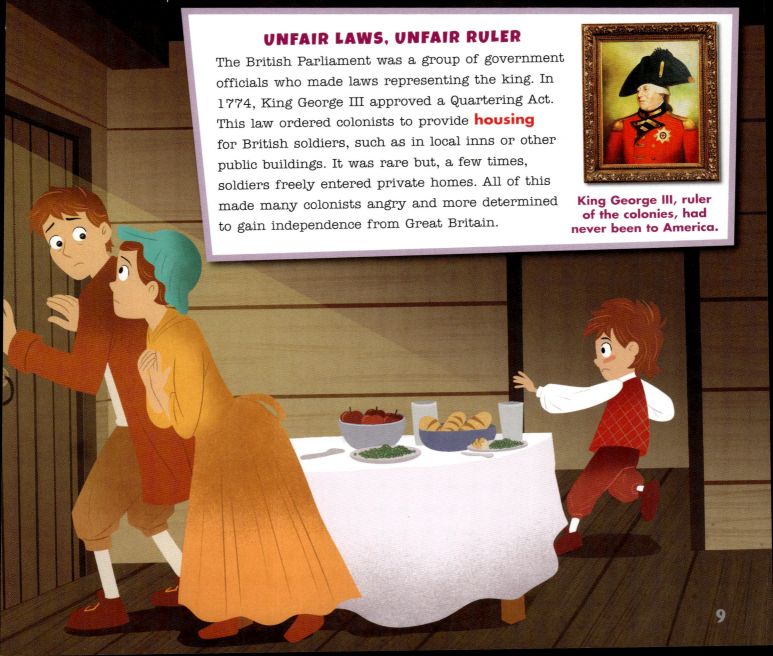

UNFAIR LAWS, UNFAIR RULER

The British Parliament was a group of government officials who made laws representing the king. In 1774, King George III approved a Quartering Act. This law ordered colonists to provide **housing** for British soldiers, such as in local inns or other public buildings. It was rare but, a few times, soldiers freely entered private homes. All of this made many colonists angry and more determined to gain independence from Great Britain.

King George III, ruler of the colonies, had never been to America.

Out of breath, Henry hurriedly explained everything to Lavinia's parents, Mr. and Mrs. Alden. Mr. Alden was furious. He was a part of the local militia.

The grown-ups comforted Henry and took him to Lavinia's room.

"Get a good night's sleep," said Mr. Alden.

Lavinia frowned. "I really hope the soldiers leave by morning," she mumbled.

"Me too!" Henry replied.

HOME, SWEET HOME

During the 18th century in colonial America, many families had farms. Less well-to-do families lived modestly in simple farmhouses much like the one pictured here. These types of houses usually had two rooms inside. There was no electricity then. There was a fireplace or two that warmed everyone in cold weather.

The roof and ceiling were made of cheap wood that eventually warped.

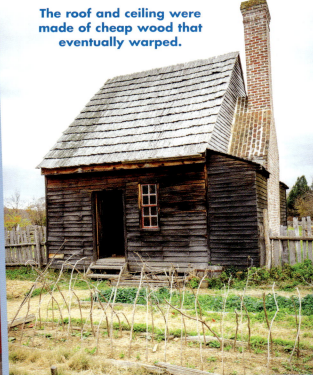

Later that night, Mr. Lewis snuck next door while the soldiers slept. He was very upset. "Those tyrants ate all our supper!" he complained to Mr. Alden. "They're already ordering us around!"

"The British will forever mistreat us," declared Mr. Alden. "We must fight for our independence as the *Common Sense* pamphlet states! That is why I joined the militia!"

Listening, Henry murmured, "We have to get the soldiers out of the house."

"Let's think of a way," Lavinia whispered.

MESSAGE IN A PAMPHLET

Thomas Paine came to Philadelphia from England in 1774. He hated Britain's unjust treatment of the colonies. In 1776, he published a pamphlet about all the reasons why America should become independent. The pamphlet was called *Common Sense*. Paine wrote plainly, so everyone could understand. His *Common Sense* message caused many colonists to think very seriously about gaining their independence.

Unlike books, pamphlets are not bound and generally don't have covers.

The next morning after breakfast, the kids had schoolwork. Henry's mother usually taught him at home. Today, Lavinia's mother taught both kids. However, Henry wasn't paying attention. He was very worried about the soldiers and wanted to go home.

Mrs. Alden noticed. "Okay, kids. You can go play," she said, smiling.

"Race you to the creek!" Lavinia said to Henry.

SCHOOL TOOLS

In colonial America, many people could not read or write. Some colonies did not have formal schools, and families taught their children at home. Schoolbooks and paper were rare and expensive. Hornbooks were common teaching tools. These were flat wooden boards. They usually had letters and numbers carved right into them.

Some hornbooks had a sheet of parchment paper with writings attached.

15

"Hey Isaac!" Henry waved to his friend near the creek.

Henry told Isaac about the soldiers.

"We want to get rid of them!" Henry exclaimed.

"One time, my parents worked in a big house folks thought was haunted," Isaac said. "People stayed away. They were scared!"

"Henry!" cried Lavinia. "If the soldiers think your farm is haunted, they could get scared off!"

Excited, the children shared ideas for scary pranks to play on the soldiers.

BLACK PEOPLE IN COLONIAL AMERICA

During colonial times, there were free African American people living in a few Northern colonies. Some owned land, homes, and businesses. However, this was uncommon. Most Black people in the colonies were **enslaved** by white people. They were treated as property and forced to work without pay. A famous line from the Declaration of Independence reads: "We hold these truths to be self-evident, that all men are created equal . . ." Yet most Black people were not treated as equals at the time.

Loyalist soldier

Patriot soldier

African American people fought on both sides of the Revolutionary War. However, some enslaved people were offered freedom if they joined the British Army. This made them more likely to band with the loyalists.

17

At nightfall, the three kids snuck next door. Everyone hid in a different spot near the outhouse.

Soon, a soldier appeared. Instantly, Lavinia ran slowly through the weeds, covered in a white blanket. "Ahhhh . . . ohhhh . . ." Henry and Isaac groaned like ghosts.

The soldier stood still, staring. "What was that?" the soldier asked, scared.

"This farm is *haaaaunted*," said Henry, with a deep voice.

Then, screaming, the soldier raced back indoors.

AN OUTDOOR TOILET

Modest colonial farmhouses did not have indoor plumbing. So, there were no bathrooms like there are today. Instead, people built outhouses outdoors. These were small wooden structures just tall enough to fit an adult standing. The toilet inside was just a wooden seat with one hole in the middle. Sometimes outhouses had more than one hole, to be used by more than one family member at a time.

Underneath the outhouse was a deep hole dug to collect waste.

The kids were not done. Later that night, they crept to the farmhouse. They heard snoring. Lavinia kept watch. Henry sat upon Isaac's shoulders, holding a fishing rod. He had tied a stick onto the handle of the rod to make it longer. Steadily, he cast the line through the open window, hooked a soldier's army jacket, and reeled it into the air. Lavinia started whispering spooky sounds. *"Uhhhh!"*

TWEEEEET! Isaac blew his whistle.

The soldiers sprang awake, staring wide-eyed at the floating coat. "Whaaaat? Th-this place is really haunted!" they stuttered.

A CONGRESS FOR CHANGE

On September 5, 1774, leaders from the 13 colonies met in Philadelphia and formed the Continental Congress. The group worked together for the good of the colonies against unfair British laws. Most **delegates** agreed that the colonies should be independent from Britain. In June 1776, a committee of five was elected to draft the Declaration of Independence. The actual writing was assigned to Thomas Jefferson, who represented the Virginia colony.

Thomas Jefferson later became the third president of the United States.

Frightened, the soldiers cried, "Let's get out of here!"

They raced out of the house as fast as they could.

Lavinia, Isaac, and Henry gave one another a huge hug to celebrate. "Hooray!" they cried.

JEFFERSON ON THE JOB

Thomas Jefferson needed a quiet place to write the Declaration. He rented two rooms at the Graff House. This was a boarding house in Philadelphia, close to where the meetings were held. Jefferson began writing on June 11, 1776. Seventeen days later, he finished the first draft of the Declaration of Independence.

This is a museum re-creation of the Graff House parlor where Jefferson wrote daily.

Henry's parents awoke to the noise. They were just in time to see the soldiers dashing away.

They were amazed at what the youngsters had managed to pull off.

"Hopefully those awful soldiers won't bother us ever again," said Mrs. Lewis.

"Now we can get our lives back to normal," Mr. Lewis said happily.

THE DECLARATION IS WRITTEN

John Adams, Benjamin Franklin, and other members of the committee rewrote parts of Jefferson's draft of the Declaration. The Declaration listed 27 **grievances** the colonists held against Great Britain. One of them was about British soldiers living in citizens' homes. The Declaration announced that the colonies were now separate and independent from British rule. The Continental Congress approved it on July 4, 1776, the date the United States celebrates as Independence Day.

John Dunlap printed the first copies—around 200—of the Declaration of Independence overnight on July 4.

One afternoon, a few days later, Henry saw a crowd of militia men rushing by. Mr. Alden, Lavinia, and Isaac were marching with them.

"Come along to Bowling Green Park to celebrate," Lavinia shouted. "The soldiers say Congress approved our Declaration of Independence!"

The Lewis family excitedly joined the parade to the park. There, the cheering crowd surrounded the huge statue of King George III on horseback—and ripped it down.

"Hurray for the Declaration!" Lavinia hollered.

"Now, we'll make our own laws," cried Henry.

"Fair laws for everyone, I hope," said Isaac.

DOWN WITH THE KING!

In 1770, a giant statue of King George III on horseback arrived from England. It was placed in Bowling Green Park in Manhattan, New York. To many colonists, it became a symbol of the British government's cruel control. On July 9, 1776, after news of the Declaration of Independence, a crowd gathered and tore down the statue.

British sculptor Joseph Wilton created the enormous lead-and-gold statue.

TIMELINE

1765 On March 22, Britain passes the Stamp Act, taxing items such as paper, books, and playing cards.

1765 On May 15, Britain passes a Quartering Act, forcing colonists to provide food and housing for British troops in their towns. Another Quartering Act will be passed nine years later, in 1774.

1768 In October, larger numbers of British troops begin arriving in America in response to growing unrest among the colonists.

1774 On September 5, the Continental Congress is formed by American leaders to address unhappiness with British rule.

1775 On April 19, the first battle of the Revolutionary War breaks out at Lexington and Concord, Massachusetts.

1776 On January 10, Thomas Paine's revolutionary pamphlet, *Common Sense*, is published.

1776 On June 11, Thomas Jefferson begins to write a draft of the Declaration of Independence.

1776 On July 4, the Declaration of Independence is approved by the Continental Congress.

1778 On February 6, French and American officials sign a military alliance against Great Britain.

1783 On September 3, the signing of the Treaty of Paris officially marks the end of the American Revolutionary War, with victory for the Americans.

WORDS TO KNOW

colonies (KAH-luh-neez) territories that have been settled by people from another country and are controlled by that country

delegate (DEL-i-git) a person sent to represent others at an assembly or conference

enslaved (en-SLAYVD) to be owned by another person and thought of as property

grievances (GREE-vuhn-suhz) strong complaints or protests

housing (HOU-zing) buildings made for people to live in

independence (in-di-PEN-duhns) the condition of not being controlled or affected by other people or things

militia (muh-LISH-uh) a group of people who are trained to fight but are not professional soldiers

Parliament (PAHR-luh-muhnt) the group of people who have been elected to make the laws in some countries

patrol (puh-TROHL) to walk or travel around an area to watch or protect it for the people within

rebel (ri-BEL) to fight against a government or against the people in charge of something

INDEX

Adams, John, 25
African Americans, 17
American Revolutionary War, 5, 8, 17, 29

British soldiers, 5, 8–9, 10, 12, 14, 16–25, 29

colonies, 5, 9, 13, 15, 17, 21, 25
Common Sense (Paine), 12–13, 29
Continental Congress, 21, 25–26, 29

Declaration of Independence, 5, 17, 21, 23, 25, 26–27, 29
delegates, 21
Dunlap, John, 25

enslaved people, 17

France, 5, 29
Franklin, Benjamin, 25

George III, King, 5, 9, 26–27
grievances, 25

housing, 9, 11, 19, 23, 25, 29

independence, 5, 9, 12–13, 21, 25

Jefferson, Thomas, 21, 23, 25, 29

laws, 5, 9, 21, 26, 29

militias, 5, 10, 12, 26

Paine, Thomas, 13, 29
Parliament, 5, 9
patrols, 8

rebels, 5

Wilton, Joseph, 27

ABOUT THE AUTHOR

Sonia W. Black has written many children's books and is strongly connected with the subject matter of this book. She was born on the Caribbean island of Jamaica, which was ruled by Great Britain for centuries. Jamaicans finally gained independence on August 6, 1962, during Queen Elizabeth II's reign. Ms. Black and her family immigrated to the United States when she was 11 years old.

ABOUT THE ILLUSTRATOR

Leo Trinidad is a *New York Times* bestselling illustrator and animator from Costa Rica. For more than 12 years, he's been creating content for children's books and TV shows. His short form series have aired in more than 40 territories around the world on channels such as Disney and Cartoon Network.